MIX
Papier aus verantwortungsvollen Quellen
Paper from responsible sources
FSC® C105338

Mihaela Butu

Shareholder Activism by Hedge Funds

Motivations and Market's Perceptions of
Hedge Fund Interventions

Butu, Mihaela: Shareholder Activism by Hedge Funds: Motivations and Market's Perceptions of Hedge Fund Interventions, Hamburg, Diplomica Verlag GmbH

Umschlaggestaltung: Diplomica Verlag GmbH, Hamburg
Covermotiv: © buchachon - Fotolia.com

ISBN: 978-3-8428-8914-9

© Diplomica Verlag GmbH, Hamburg 2013

Bibliografische Information der Deutschen Nationalbibliothek:

Die Deutsche Nationalbibliothek verzeichnet diese Publikation in der Deutschen Nationalbibliografie; detaillierte bibliografische Daten sind im Internet über http://dnb.d-nb.de abrufbar.

Die digitale Ausgabe (eBook-Ausgabe) dieses Titels trägt die ISBN 978-3-8428-3914-4 und kann über den Handel oder den Verlag bezogen werden.

Dieses Werk ist urheberrechtlich geschützt. Die dadurch begründeten Rechte, insbesondere die der Übersetzung, des Nachdrucks, des Vortrags, der Entnahme von Abbildungen und Tabellen, der Funksendung, der Mikroverfilmung oder der Vervielfältigung auf anderen Wegen und der Speicherung in Datenverarbeitungsanlagen, bleiben, auch bei nur auszugsweiser Verwertung, vorbehalten. Eine Vervielfältigung dieses Werkes oder von Teilen dieses Werkes ist auch im Einzelfall nur in den Grenzen der gesetzlichen Bestimmungen des Urheberrechtsgesetzes der Bundesrepublik Deutschland in der jeweils geltenden Fassung zulässig. Sie ist grundsätzlich vergütungspflichtig. Zuwiderhandlungen unterliegen den Strafbestimmungen des Urheberrechtes. Die Wiedergabe von Gebrauchsnamen, Handelsnamen, Warenbezeichnungen usw. in diesem Werk berechtigt auch ohne besondere Kennzeichnung nicht zu der Annahme, dass solche Namen im Sinne der Warenzeichen- und Markenschutz-Gesetzgebung als frei zu betrachten wären und daher von jedermann benutzt werden dürften. Die Informationen in diesem Werk wurden mit Sorgfalt erarbeitet. Dennoch können Fehler nicht vollständig ausgeschlossen werden und die Diplomica GmbH, die Autoren oder Übersetzer übernehmen keine juristische Verantwortung oder irgendeine Haftung für evtl. verbliebene fehlerhafte Angaben und deren Folgen.

Vorwort

Sehr geehrter Leser,

im Jahre 2010 entschloss sich der Bundesverband Alternative Investments e. V. (BAI), wissenschaftliche Arbeiten im Bereich der sog. Alternativen Investments zu fördern. Zu diesem Zweck wurde damals der BAI-Wissenschaftspreis ins Leben gerufen.

Einer der Hauptgründe sowie die Intention für diese Förderung waren und sind, dass das Wissen über Alternative Investments sowohl in der Breite als auch in der Tiefe leider immer noch sehr rudimentär ist. In weiten Teilen der Öffentlichkeit, der Politik, der Medien, aber auch auf Seiten der Investoren herrschen oftmals vielfache Missverständnisse hinsichtlich Nutzen und Risiken von Alternative Investments. Mit dem Wissenschaftspreis will der BAI einen Anreiz für Studenten und Wissenschaftler in Deutschland schaffen, Forschungsarbeit in diesem für institutionelle Investoren zukünftig immer wichtiger werdenden Bereich zu leisten.

Viele deutsche Hochschulen erklärten sich auf Anhieb bereit, den BAI bei der Bekanntmachung des Wissenschaftspreises zu unterstützen. Daraus resultierend erreichten den BAI zahlreiche anspruchsvolle Bewerbungen in den vier Kategorien „Dissertationen", „Master-/Diplomarbeiten", „Bachelorarbeiten" und „Sonstige Wissenschaftliche Arbeiten". Für diese wurde jährlich neben einem Award ein Preisgeld von 10.000 Euro an die Gewinner ausgelobt.

Wir freuen uns sehr, dass der Diplomica Verlag die Reihe „Alternative Investments" ins Leben gerufen hat. Diese Publikation wird sicherlich auch dazu beitragen, das Thema Alternative Investments einer Vielzahl von Personen näherzubringen.

Wir wünschen dem Leser nun eine spannende Lektüre!

Ihr
Bundesverband Alternative Investments e. V.

Abstract

Hedge funds have effectively become important players in the corporate governance of public companies, causing, contrariwise, much polemic in public opinion. This paper analyses the nature of hedge fund activism in the United States using a data set of SEC filings for the period from 1994 to 2006. The paper assesses various types of activism in the context of hedge fund activists' approaches to targeted firms. Hedge funds only occasionally seek control over their targets and less hostile types of activism prevail. The positive market reaction around the announcement of hedge fund interventions indicates the favourable impact of activism on target companies' value. The announcement returns on more aggressive types of activism are larger, which may be associated with hedge funds' bargaining power in respect of firms' management in accomplishing the objectives of their interventions. The reasons for hedge funds' ability to perform effective monitoring may lie in their unique organisational structure and regulatory framework.

Table of contents

Vorwort 5

Abstract 7

List of figures 10

List of tables 11

1 Introduction 13

2 Shareholder Activism 17
   2.1 Activism by traditional institutions 17
   2.2 Activism by hedge funds 18

3 Data and overview of types of activism 21
   3.1 The sample 21
   3.2 Classification of events by type of activism 23
   3.3 Examples of activist events 28

4 Stock returns on hedge fund activism 33
   4.1 Methodology 33
   4.2 Empirical results 35
      4.2.1 Abnormal returns by years 35
      4.2.2 Abnormal returns by type of activism 38

5 Summary and conclusion 41

Appendix: Two examples of activist events – Schedule 13D 43

References 53

List of figures

Figure 1: Distribution of hedge fund and non hedge fund events.. 23
Figure 2: Distribution of events by type of activism 28
Figure 3: Cumulative abnormal returns around activism filing... 37

List of tables

Table 1: Events by year 22
Table 2: Events by type of activism 25
Table 3: Cumulative abnormal returns by years 36
Table 4: Cumulative abnormal returns by type of activism 39

1 Introduction

For more than two decades shareholder activism has been part of the United States' corporate governance landscape, affecting legal and financial decisions. This phenomenon generated a prompt academic response resulting in a series of empirical research contributions trying to assess the real impact of shareholder interventions. Yet, the views on whether shareholder activism enhances the value of target firms are mixed. The positive assessment of investor activism is based on the belief that it can provide an effective monitoring of the management of publicly listed companies, reducing agency costs. The logic of this conviction is based on the fact that institutional shareholders, owning large blocks, have an incentive to develop specialized expertise in assessing and monitoring investments (Bainbridge, 2005) and they are able "to absorb the costs of watching the management" (Shleifer & Vishny, 1986, p. 462). These features, coupled with their voting power, enable them to intervene and to initiate changes in the companies when they perform poorly or when the maximization of shareholder value is not pursued. On the other hand, there is increasingly more evidence suggesting that "shareholder activism, in general, has little effect on the target firm's values, earnings, or operations" (Song & Szewczyk, 2003, p. 318) and that it "will not solve the principal-agent problem [...] but rather will shift the focus on that problem" (Bainbridge, 2005, p. 1). Furthermore Romano claims that the empirical literature "presents an apparent paradox: Notwithstanding commentators' generally positive assessment of the development of such shareholder activism, the empirical studies suggest that it has an insignificant effect on targeted firms' performance" and some studies find "a significant negative stock price effect from activism" (Romano, 2001, p. 4).

However, it seems that the "playing field" of activism has changed and actors other than the pension and mutual funds are increasingly involved in activism, namely hedge funds. Hedge funds are considered to have better incentives to monitor a company's management and board than other financial intermediaries, due to their unique organizational structure (Clifford, 2008). The critical role played by hedge funds in corporate governance is reflected by their involvement in some large companies that have captured public attention. Thus, in 2005 McDonald's became a target of activist hedge funds who pressured the management to spin-off 65% of company-owned restaurants and borrow USD 14.7 billion against its real estate (CFO, 2005). In the same year, the prominent hedge fund manager Carl Icahn asked Time Warner to split the company's component businesses, to initiate a USD 20 billion share buyback and then started a proxy fight against the management (SEC, 2005; CNN Money, 2006). And finally, hedge funds opposed the acquisition of the remaining 58% stake in Chiron Corporation by Novartis, in 2006 (SEC, 2006; CNN Money, 2006).

Although shareholder activism in general and hedge fund activism in particular were not an issue on the German corporate market, no later than 2005 hedge fund activism became a subject of public attention. It was in the case of the German Stock Exchange's attempt to acquire the London Stock Exchange, which failed (for the second time) because of the opposition of the London-based hedge fund, The Children's Investment Fund Management (TCI). The fund argued that the transaction would not enhance shareholder value and instead the Exchange should buy shares back (Kahan & Rock, 2006). TCI was then supported by Atticus Capital who "accused the exchange of "empire building" at the expense of its shareholders" (Financial Times, 2005). This marks the moment when German public opinion became aware of the potential influence of hedge fund activists and they received the epithet "locust" (The Economist, 2009).

Even though the hedge fund industry was weakened by losses and cash outflows as a result of the late-2000s financial crisis, since 2009 hedge funds seem to have developed new interest for German companies and made investments in Rheinmetall (Greenlight Capital), HeidelbergCement (Paulson & Co.) and Gerresheimer (Sageview Capital, Pennant Capital, Eton Park, Brett Barakett) without revealing the purposes of their investments (Böhm & Grote, 2009). Yet, there are few empirical studies which focus on effects of hedge fund activism on the German market in particular.

Since hedge funds are able to influence decision making in publicly listed companies, the public opinion of hedge fund activism is controversial. The main criticism is based on the accusation of short-termism and value destruction by distracting managers from long-term projects (Kahan & Rock, 2006). However, recent empirical studies (e.g., Brav, Jiang, Thomas, & Partnoy, 2008; Clifford, 2008; Klein and Zur, 2009) show the opposite, arguing that hedge funds may be able to perform better monitoring of management, leading to a reduction in agency costs and thus creating value at the target firms.

While this paper is not able to clarify this dispute, it analyses the proposals made by hedge funds when acquiring large shares of voting rights in listed companies, for a better understanding of the motivations behind hedge funds' activism and the market's perception of interventions. More precisely, this study addresses some of the main questions regarding shareholder activism performed by hedge funds: How does the market react to the announcement of activism? Does hedge fund activism create value in target firms? What type of activism are hedge funds performing, or, in other words, what types of demand do hedge funds bring forward and how does the market assess them?

In addressing these questions the announcements of activism by hedge funds in the United States are analysed in a time period between 1994 and 1996. As soon as a hedge fund surpasses the 5% ownership threshold in a publicly traded company, it must file a regulatory disclosure with the U.S. Securities and Exchange Commission (SEC). Investors who intend to influence the firm or who have future plans to do so file a Schedule 13D, thus signalling their activist intentions. Consequently, the first indication of the impact of hedge fund activism is derived from the market's reaction to these filings. The findings show that the market responds positively to activism, resulting in average abnormal stock returns of 2.18% within a short 20-day interval around the announcement. These results are in line with evidence provided by Greenwood and Schor (2009) and Clifford (2008), who observed 3.61% and

3.39%, respectively, excess returns surrounding the filing date. Scholars like Brav et al. (2008) find much larger abnormal returns of over 7% during the announcement window.

The positive market reaction indicates value creation in the target firms, at least in short-term consideration, which could be a result of favourable expectations regarding the implementation of operational, financial, or governance-related changes demanded by activists. From a long-term perspective, Brav et al. (2008) document an increase in leverage and total payout ratio following activism, which is consistent with a reduction of the agency costs associated with free cash flow and increased market discipline. An alternative hypothesis is provided by Greenwood and Schor, who relate the high returns around the announcement of activism to the "investor's expectations that the target firms will be acquired at a premium to the current stock price" (Greenwood & Schor, 2009, p. 2).

Finally, based on the information disclosed in schedule 13D, this paper identifies the types of activism that hedge funds conduct and evaluates the market's perception of each of them. The first observation is the large heterogeneity in activists' set of demands and objectives of engagement towards target companies. Moreover, there is evidence showing that the more aggressive the activism is, the larger the positive abnormal returns are. Thus, funds revealing their attempts to acquire control of the targets are associated with the largest positive abnormal returns of 11.30%, whereas demanding the sale of the companies or their main assets to a third party results in 3.23% excess returns. One feature distinguishing this paper from the main empirical studies on types of activism is that it classifies the demands for asset sale and the attempts of hedge funds to acquire a company into two distinct groups, that way trying to better capture the motives and the hostility of activists. By contrast, scholars like Greenwood and Schor, Brav et al., and Clifford do not make this distinction, considering the demands for asset sales and takeover efforts of the funds as one single category. Thus, Brav et al. (2008) and Greenwood and Schor (2009) suggest that the request for sale of the company is associated with the largest positive abnormal returns of 8.54% and 6.83%, respectively. As the authors do not distinguish the effects of abnormal returns, it might be possible that much of the gains are driven by the takeover intentions of the activist hedge funds. Further, large positive abnormal returns of 3.58% are also reported when activists try to block a merger, which is in line with findings made by Greenwood and Schor, who relate 5.91% excess returns.

Although announcement of activists' intentions to engage in proxy contest with targets' management is a further hostile tactic performed by activist hedge funds, the results provided for this type of activism are not able to support the above mentioned hypothesis as the findings show negative average abnormal returns of -1.04%. In contrast, Greenwood and Schor show large positive abnormal returns of 4.56% associated with this category of activism. Similarly negative is the market's assessment of activism that targets firms' capital structure – including recapitalization, dividends and share repurchases – resulting in -3.71% abnormal returns. These results are consistent with the main literature that reports insignificant returns on this type of activism.

The importance of the subject arises especially from a political perspective, since activism by hedge funds is generally viewed with scepticism. As this paper will show, hedge funds, despite their generally more aggressive style of performing shareholder activism, are not typically interested in taking over control of their targets. These findings also represent an essential element for distinguishing between the role of hedge funds and traditional corporate raiders of the 1980s in the US corporate governance landscape. Moreover, activist hedge funds can be viewed as a middle ground between internal monitoring by traditional institutional investors and external monitoring by corporate raiders which puts hedge funds in a possibly unique position to reduce agency costs (Brav et al., 2008). The evidence of a positive market assessment of activism by hedge funds challenges the recent calls for increased regulation, as it could make activism less attractive.

The rest of the paper proceeds as follows. The next section provides the institutional background of shareholder activism, emphasizing hedge funds peculiarities as activist shareholders. The third section describes the sample and the types of activism. The fourth section presents the results and discusses the market's reaction to hedge fund activism. And finally, the paper is rounded off by some conclusions.

2 Shareholder Activism

2.1 Activism by traditional institutions

The history of shareholder activism starts in the middle 1980s and emerges as a response to developments in the United States corporate control market. In consequence of the abrogation of restrictive takeover laws in many U.S. states in 1982, many company managers sought out new takeover defences to secure control over their firms. Some of the new defensive tools included antitakeover charter amendments, poison pills and restrictive state antitakeover laws. Hence, by the late 1980s the majority of the firms had adopted such measures and created huge obstacles to hostile takeover attempts. This also implied that "some existing capital market mechanisms for replacing firm managers had almost stopped functioning" (Karpoff, Malatesta, & Walkling, 1996, p. 368). Consequently, many dispersed individual investors started to submit shareholder proposals on corporate governance, including proposals to eliminate defensive tactics against takeovers or to enhance board independence (Romano, 2001). At the same time, large institutional investors, like pension and mutual funds, began their activist involvement in corporate policies using Rule 14a-8.[1] These proposals were precatory resolutions and related to various corporate governance issues, such as poison pills, confidential voting, and board structure, rather than to specific aspects of a firm's business or management (Kahan & Rock, 2006).

However, the views on benefits of this type of activism are mixed. Shleifer and Vishny (1986) document the fact that large shareholders may be able to effectively monitor the management of listed companies, thus providing a solution to the free-rider problem. Among other factors, they show that large shareholders used takeover mechanisms to discipline the management, which was possible, however, only in the years without the above-mentioned antitakeover measures. On the other hand, a competing view sustains the idea that shareholder proposals made by traditional institutions are unlikely to cause significant policy changes or have any valuable effect on firm performance (Karpoff, Malatesta, & Walkling, (1996), Black (1998), Romano (2001).

Just as the success of activism by hedge funds is attributed to their unique organizational structure, so the failure of value-increasing activism is explained by the organizational characteristics of traditional institutional investors. Institutional investors, like public pension funds and mutual funds, are subject to regulatory and structural constraints that limit their scope of shareholder activism. Accordingly, Black (1990) argues that mutual funds, for instance, face conflicts of interests because many of them manage the corporate pension plans and thus have business ties with portfolio companies that would be jeopardized by activism. As institutions widely open to the public, mutual and pension funds are regulated by the Investment Company Act of 1940, which imposes a series of further restrictions. For instance,

---

[1] "Rule 14a-8 provides an opportunity for a shareholder owning a relatively small amount of a company's securities to have his or her proposal placed alongside management's proposals in that company's proxy materials for presentation to a vote at an annual or special meeting of shareholders" (SEC, 2001)

they are subject to diversification requirements that make concentrated ownership in a single company impossible. This is important because only large holdings of voting rights enable shareholders to put pressure on management and pursue individual requirements. Additionally, they have restrictions on shorting, borrowing, and investing in illiquid securities (Brav et al., 2008). The fund managers of traditional institutions lack significant personal financial incentives to engage in interventions, since they have restrictions on charging substantial performance fees (Rock, 1991). Given all these constraints, Clifford argues that "activist threats by pensions and mutual funds are not viewed as credible by target firm management, and therefore the market" (Clifford, 2008, p. 325), making a reduction in agency costs doubtful.

2.2 Activism by hedge funds

On the contrary, given their organizational characteristics and regulatory environment, hedge funds could be more appropriate institutions to effectively perform shareholder activism. Hedge funds became a major corporate governance phenomenon in the mid-2000s (Armour & Cheffins, 2009) and "are likely to remain an important and controversial feature of the legal and financial landscape for some time to come" (Macey, 2008, as cited in Armour & Cheffins, 2009, p. 1). Hedge funds are pooled, privately organized investment vehicles, not available to the general public and, importantly, avoid the Investment Company Act of 1940 by having a small number of sophisticated investors (Brav et al., 2008). Hedge funds are not required by law to maintain high levels of diversification and therefore, they can take much larger positions in one single company. Hedge funds are usually not bound by liquidity constraints and are able to "lock-up" their funds for extended periods of two years or longer (Kahan & Rock, 2006). This feature is important insofar as some activist campaigns may require the holding of large, illiquid positions for longer periods of time. Furthermore, since hedge funds are permitted to apply much higher leverage and to make use of derivative instruments, they can acquire significant effective ownership in target companies (Clifford, 2008).

An important characteristic of hedge funds is the manager's strong incentive structure. Typically, hedge funds charge a fixed annual fee of 2% of their assets and a performance fee of 20% of the fund's annualized returns. Given this remuneration structure, hedge fund managers have much greater incentives to conduct value-increasing activism, despite the high costs of intervention (Kahan & Rock, 2006; Clifford, 2008). Additionally, Brav et al. (2008) argue that the fund managers undergo less conflict of interest than managers of traditional investment institutions, as they do not sell financial products to the firms whose shares they hold.

Finally, hedge funds are considered to have higher negotiating power with the firm's management, due to their ability to acquire the company if they are dissatisfied with the operating or governing competence of management. In most cases, however, hedge funds use these threats as a tactical tool, while they seldom follow through with the takeover transaction.

Clifford (2008) shows that funds which have threatened to buy out a company often reach arrangements with the firm's management and achieve all or some of their stipulated demands. Thus, unlike traditional institutions, hedge funds represent a credible threat to their targets and make activism efforts more effective.

Characterizing hedge fund-style activism, Armour and Cheffins (2009) describe it as "offensive" shareholder activism, in the sense that hedge funds lacking a significant stake in a company acquire one "offensively" assuming that valuation failures will be corrected to maximize shareholder returns and with the intention of press management to make changes if it opposes doing so. In contrast, the "defensive" activism performed by other institutional investors aims to protect through intervention the shares already held. Hence hedge funds, rather than investing and passively waiting for the market to self-correct, take the initiative by agitating the management for changes in order to boost shareholder value. Similarly, Kahan and Rock describe the different approach to activist intervention adopted by hedge funds and traditional institutional investors as follows:

"Mutual fund and public pension fund activism, if it occurs, tends to be intermittent and ex post: when fund management notes that portfolio companies are underperforming, or that their governance regime is deficient, they will sometimes become active. In contrast, hedge fund activism is strategic and ex ante: hedge fund managers first determine whether a company would benefit from activism, then take a position, and then become active. It represents a blurring of the line between risk arbitrage and battles over corporate strategy and control" (Kahan & Rock, 2006, p. 35).

Viewed from the perspective of efficient market theory, hedge fund activists appear to "exploit market inefficiency and generate superior returns if and when prices return to fundamental values" (Allen, Myers, & Brealey, 2008, p. 369). In this case market inefficiency is associated with information asymmetry, bad management and other agency related problems. Further, some authors (Brav et al., 2008) interpret activist investing as a new form of arbitrage, maintaining that in efficient markets, abnormal returns on activist investing should persist only when an activist has superior information about the value of the firm that is supposed to be out of the control of the investors and unknown to the market. Interventions by activist investors could potentially affect the value of the firm by their action. Consequently, the announcement of activists' investments in a company may signal to the market their private information about the value of the targeted firms. In general, this kind of arbitrage activity can make markets more efficient as market prices reflect additional information.

Given all the distinguishing features of hedge fund activism mentioned above, it appears that they are the new forces of corporate influence (rather than control, as evidence will show later on) and as long as their gains exceed the cost of interventions, they will have sufficient incentive to engage in activism. The next step is therefore to see how exactly hedge funds proceed when engaging in activism.

3 Data and overview of types of activism

3.1 The sample

The sample analysed is based mostly on Schedule 13D filed with the U.S. Securities and Exchange Commission for the period between 1994 and 2006. Schedule 13D is a mandatory federal securities law filing under the Section 13(d) of the Securities Exchange Act of 1934 which states that investors must file within ten days of acquiring more than 5% of a voting class of a publicly traded company's equity securities (SEC, 2008). The filing documents the investor's company name and all its affiliated parties (the reporting persons), the size of the purchased shareholding as well as investor's intentions. Filing a Schedule 13D is a notification of activist intentions per se, because passive investors who do not have any intent to influence the target companies and are not going to have these intentions in the future file a Schedule 13G when acquiring more than 5%, but less than 10%, of the company's stock. Schedule 13G is shorter and requires less information from the filing party. If an investor changes its initial passive intentions and decides to become active, it must file a Schedule 13D (Brav, Jiang, Thomas, & Partnoy, 2008). In addition, any material changes in the fund's purposes contained in the initial schedule, require prompt disclosure in a subsequent amendment (Schedule 13D/A).

To the sample of 13Ds and amendments on 13Ds are also added the definitive and preliminary proxy statements filed by non-management (DFAN14A and PREC14A). These statements under Section 14(a) of the Securities Exchange Act of 1934 are filed with the SEC by investors who intend to be or are involved in a proxy fight with a company's management. Form DFAN14A is defined as "Additional definitive proxy soliciting materials filed by non-management" and is filed ahead of the annual shareholder meeting when soliciting shareholders vote. This form identifies the party taking action, the investment position held in the company, the action to be taken and the preferred results of such action. The purpose of this filing is to ensure that information is timely distributed to all shareholders, since its intended result is to force a change not proposed by the registrant (SEC, 2011) Form PREC14A is also known as "Preliminary proxy statements - contested solicitations" and must be filed by or on behalf of a registrant when a shareholder vote is required on a contested solicitation. The intention of this filing is to provide security holders with the information necessary to permit them to make an informed vote at the upcoming annual shareholder's meeting or to authorize a proxy to vote on their behalf (SEC, 2011). A proxy contest may be initiated with less than a 5% stake in the target companies' shares. The reason for including these filings in the sample is the fact that activist hedge funds use proxy statements as a tactical instrument to achieve the goals often stated previously in their Schedules 13D, since the mean owning stake in the target companies of funds filing the proxy statements of the sample is 9.88%.

With very large companies certain hedge funds may engage in activism when they own less than 5% of the firms' shares. The sample contains three such cases. The most remarkable example is the activism performed by Carl Icahn, who owned only 2.6% of shares in Time

Warner, when he started the fight against the firm in 2005. Other examples are the activism by Pirate Capital with 1.6% ownership in Mirant Corporation and the activist engagement of Accipiter Capital Management with a 3.5% stake in Arena Pharmaceuticals.

Thus the initial sample, retrieved from SEC EDGAR database, includes a total of 622 filings. The corresponding target companies' data and the stock prices are collected from the CRSP database. The initial data contains filings made by both hedge funds and non-hedge funds, which are identified with a dummy variable. This leads to 496 filings registered by hedge fund activists and 126 by non-hedge funds. From these, multiple filings for a target company are excluded by taking the earliest filing date. Hence, for each activist - target pair there is only one event. The final sample comprises a total of 597 filings, 474 of them filed by hedge funds and 123 by non-hedge fund activists. Table 1 summarizes the sample, indicating the number of events for each year.

Table 1: Events by year

Year	Hedge Fund	Non-Hedge Fund	Total
1994	4	1	5
1995	5	2	7
1996	14	6	20
1997	32	14	46
1998	37	13	50
1999	34	16	50
2000	43	10	53
2001	34	15	49
2002	39	17	56
2003	31	7	38
2004	37	11	48
2005	79	6	85
2006	85	5	90
Total	**474**	**123**	**597**

This table provides an overview of the number of events for each year between 1994 and 2006. An event is defined as the filing date of Schedule 13D (or DFAN14A or PREC14A) announcing 5% or more ownership and the intention to influence the management of the target company or its business course. It shows the total number of events as well as the number of events filed by hedge funds and non-hedge funds separately.

The number of hedge fund related events increased almost monotonically during the observed period of time, from 4 events in 1994 to 85 events in 2006. Over the entire sample nearly five times more hedge funds engaged in activism using 13D filings than other institutional investors did. A better visual illustration of the distribution of activist filings over the sample period is provided by Figure 1. The table above, as well as the figure, reveal that the number of hedge fund filings relative to non-hedge fund filings rose dramatically in later sample years, 2005 and 2006, respectively. The same trends are shown in the empirical research of Greenwood and Schor (2009), who analysed activist filings over the same time period.

Figure 1: Distribution of hedge fund and non hedge fund events

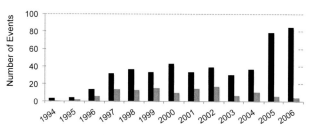

The figure shows the distribution of hedge fund and non-hedge fund events from 1994 until 2006. The entire sample covers 597 filings which are distributed into 474 filings registered by activist hedge funds and 123 by non-hedge funds.

The 474 events were initiated by 137 different hedge funds, of these 61 were serial activists (i.e., hedge funds file a Schedule 13D more than once within the sample) and 76 non-serial activists. The most frequent activist hedge funds with more than 10 filings within the sample and constituting almost half of it (46.6%) are: Blum Capital Partners, Cannell Capital, Farallon Capital Management, Greenway Partners, Carl Icahn, David Nierenberg, Pirate Capital, Steel Partner, Third Point, VA Partners and Wynnefield Partners.

3.2 Classification of events by type of activism

In order to understand what type of activism hedge funds are performing, the stated purposes of intervention of all 474 filings are analysed. Every Schedule 13D as well as the amendments on Schedule 13D include under Item 4 a "Purpose of Transaction", in which the filer must disclose any proposals or requests that could result in a substantial change in the target company. Such proposals may concern, for instance, the election of new members to the Board of Directors, a recommendation for a stock repurchase program or even a bid to acquire the target. Often, investors have no current plans to influence the company, acquiring shares of the targets for "investment purposes", but file a Schedule 13D to reserve the right to affect the firm or its management in the future. In addition to information contained in the section "Purpose of Transaction", the filings 13D are often accompanied by supplementary materials as exhibits. These exhibits may contain joint filing agreements (in cases when multiple funds join together), letters to the company's management or Board of Directors and even lawsuit filings against the company. These additional materials and the remarks in 13D provide the market with very detailed information about the activist's intentions regarding the target. As Clifford (2008) argues, the importance of detailed and truthful statements arises from the evidence that the SEC and target companies will otherwise utilize the court system to enforce correct disclosure by investors. Hence, managers of firms targeted by activist hedge funds often use apparent misstatements in the investor's 13D filing as a basis for lawsuits. Hedge funds, being aware of the generally negative attitude that firm management and public opinion have towards them, are extremely careful when filing the Schedule 13D in order to avoid ambiguous disclosures.

The stated objectives that activist hedge funds provide when announcing their active involvement in the target firms can be classified into ten distinct categories, labelled as follows: 1) engage management, 2) corporate governance, 3) asset sale, 4) capital structure, 5) block a merger or an acquisition, 6) business strategy, 7) strategic alternatives, 8) takeover bid, 9) proxy contest and 10) financing.[2] The demands are not mutually exclusive as one event can be assigned to multiple categories. For example, if the activist requests a stock buyback program and seeks the election of its own nominees to the board of directors of the target company, then this event falls under categories two and three. Table 2 summarizes all categories indicating the number of events for each set of demands per year and the fraction of each category relative to the whole sample.

---

[2] With exception of takeover bid, the names of categories are based on the work of Greenwood & Schor, 2009.

Table 2: Events by type of activism

Year	Engage Management	Corporate Governance	Asset Sale	Capital Structure	Block Merger	Business Strategy	Strategic Alternatives	Takeover Bid	Proxy Contest	Financing
1994	2	3	1	1	-	-	-	1	-	-
1995	2	1	-	-	-	-	-	-	-	-
1996	7	3	2	-	3	-	-	-	1	-
1997	18	5	3	3	-	1	2	3	1	1
1998	19	7	10	3	2	2	2	-	-	-
1999	17	8	6	4	-	1	1	1	3	1
2000	23	9	9	4	1	1	2	3	2	-
2001	20	8	4	5	-	2	3	-	-	1
2002	14	9	9	6	1	4	2	4	2	1
2003	15	11	5	1	-	-	1	1	-	-
2004	18	8	2	5	2	4	2	4	1	1
2005	35	18	9	10	9	5	3	4	2	-
2006	38	23	14	7	8	2	4	3	7	1
Total	**228**	**113**	**74**	**52**	**27**	**22**	**22**	**21**	**20**	**5**
% of all Events	39.0%	19.3%	12.7%	8.9%	4.6%	3.8%	3.8%	3.6%	3.4%	0.9%

This table reports the summary of events by activist hedge funds' demands for each year between 1994 and 2006. The reported objectives can be classified into ten distictive categories. Since the categories are non-exclusive, the number of events in each category sum to more than 474. The table shows the total number of events for each category as well as the fraction of each category relative to the entire sample.

The results reveal that the most frequent objective of activist hedge funds, representing 39.0% of the full sample, or 228 filings, is to engage in discussions with companies' management in order to enhance shareholder value. In some cases, activists make only a general statement that shares are undervalued without indicating a specific course of action. This category also includes those filings where the activist funds have no other present purposes than investment. As already mentioned above, activists choose to file a Schedule 13D instead of 13G to reserve the right to engage in future activism. The usual phrasing in such cases is:

"The Reporting Persons have acquired the Issuer's Common Stock for investment purposes. [...] Consistent with its investment research methods and evaluation criteria, the Reporting Persons may discuss such matters with management or directors of the Issuer, other shareholders, industry analysts. [...] The Reporting Persons *reserve the right* to formulate other plans and/or make other proposals, and take such actions with respect to their investment in the Issuer" (SEC, 2005).

Corporate governance related matters are expressed in 113 filings representing 19.3% and are, therefore, the second largest category in the sample. The demands of this category relate to the election of one's own nominees to the board of directors, removal of certain incumbent members of the board, calls for the board's independence, replacement of existing members of the management, or removal of poison pills. The corporate governance classification also includes activism that targets management incentive plans and compensation programs, corporate fraud and directors' violation of fiduciary duties. Sometimes activist hedge funds communicate their satisfaction and support of the current management, although this is rare.

A more aggressive type of activism is asset sale, represented by 74 filings, or 12.7%, where activist hedge funds urge the sale of the entire company or certain assets to a third party as a means of enhancing shareholder value. Often, activists recommend a merger partner for the targets.

Activists targeting capital structure related issues account for 8.9% of the sample, or a total of 52 filings. This type of activism includes requirements regarding recapitalization, higher payouts to shareholders using dividend payback or stock repurchases, reduction of excess cash, stock or debt issuance, debt restructuring or opposition to some restructuring measures that would involve a dilution of their shares.

Another hostile type of activism is represented by activists' efforts to block a merger with another firm or a management buyout, usually because they consider the terms of the transaction unfavourable to the companies' shareholders. This category corresponds to 27 filings, or 4.6% of the sample. In most cases, activists also announce their intentions to vote against the merger at an upcoming shareholder meeting. Typically, activists use this tactic to increase the bid made for the target. As some authors suggest (Partnoy & Thomas, 2005), this type of activism may be linked to an anti-merger strategy, where hedge funds take a position that would benefit when the intended merger collapsed and then strategically vote against the merger.

Activists motivated by business strategy related topics cover 22 filings, or 3.8% of the sample. In many cases, hedge funds criticize operational inefficiencies and unprofitable business segments, level of investment in some business lines or lack of business focus. Furthermore, activists often demand the reduction of operating expenses or of risk in some business lines, call for improvement of profitability ratios, encourage the company's reduction in cash-burn rate or revenue growth.

Strategic alternatives issues are demanded in 22 filings of the sample, representing 3.8%. This classification consists of requests to spin-off target companies' underperforming divisions, to seek a strategic joint venture, to separate business divisions in order to focus on core competencies, to expand existing operations or contains recommendations on strategic acquisitions of new businesses as part of a growth strategy to be pursued.

Further, the sample reveals that 3.6% of the total number of filings, or 21 events, represent an offer by the activist itself to acquire the target company. In pursuing takeover attempts, hedge funds usually announce their intentions in a non-aggressive manner, but whenever the target companies' management is not responsive, they threaten a proxy contest and make the tender offer directly to the targets' shareholders in an upcoming annual meeting. An example of tender offer phrasing is illustrated in Schedule 13D under the Item 4 "Purpose of Transaction" filed by Highfields Capital Management: "[…] based upon publicly available information, Highfields Capital is prepared to pursue an acquisition of all of the outstanding common shares of Circuit City for $17.00 in cash. This offer represents a premium of over 20% both to last night's close and the average closing price of Circuit's City shares for the last twenty trading days" (SEC, 2005).

Another set of events is constituted by the filings under Schedule 14A (DFAN14A and PREC14A), where activists indicate their intention to solicit proxies from shareholders at the companies' annual meeting. The total number of filings is 20, corresponding to 3.4% of the sample. By launching a proxy contest, activist hedge funds tend to solicit proxies in support of the election of their own nominees or independent directors to the board, asking shareholders to vote against approval of a merger agreement or even to help "to press the company to take more aggressive steps to increase shareholder value" (SEC, 2000).

Finally, the least represented type of activism is financing, with only 5 events, or 0.9% of the entire sample. This category includes hedge funds' intentions to provide financing to the target companies, related whether to funding the targets' growth or acquisition strategies, refinancing the indebtedness, facilitating an interest payment or sometimes providing additional working capital.

Figure 2 is a graphical representation of the distribution of events by activism type discussed above. It illustrates where the main focus of hedge funds is, when involved in activism, namely to engage in discussions with target companies' management in order to increase shareholder value. This category is one of the less aggressive (alongside with providing financing to the targets) in the entire sample, hinting at the assumption that hedge funds, despite their frequently aggressive behavior, do not typically pursue to take over control of targets when performing shareholder activism, as is generally believed. Additional evidence on this subject will be provided later on in this paper.

Figure 2: Distribution of events by type of activism

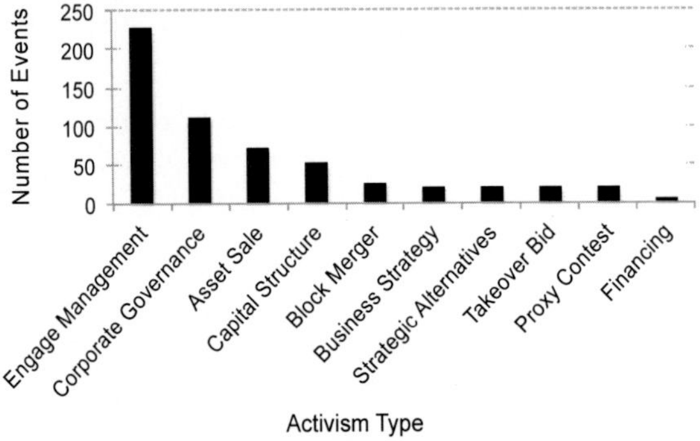

The figure illustrates the distribition of events by type of demands. The objectives, indicated in Schedule 13D, and the filings under the Schedule 14A, can be classified in ten well-defined categories. The categories are non-exclusive, as one event may fall under multiple categories.

Reading the statements filed by activist hedge funds revealed not only how detailed the filings must be, but also how accurately hedge fund managers analyse and monitor their targets. The specific demands regarding capital structure, profitability ratios or working capital show that hedge fund managers have an excellent command of balance sheet and income statement analysis. In support of this idea, Armour and Cheffins argue that hedge funds that engage in offensive shareholder activism rely on diligent analysis of corporate fundamentals. Accordingly, activist hedge fund managers "tend not to be experts in quantitative theories of finance – the typical qualification of a hedge fund manager – but are often former investment bankers or research analysts used to working hard to understand balance sheets and income statements" (Armour & Cheffins, 2009, p. 4).

3.3 Examples of activist events

Describing the ten types of hedge fund activism in the previous section, short citations from Schedule 13D filings were occasionally included for a better understanding of the categories where more explanation was needed. In the following section, a more precise idea of the activism that this paper focus on is provided by a description of two such cases retrieved from the sample. The first event exemplifies a non-aggressive and friendly approach that the target's management subsequently embraced. The second event illustrates a more aggressive and confrontational position that was also ultimately accepted by the company's management. These examples illustrate the two extremes of activism: the friendly and the aggressive, but the sample also contains more impersonal and neutral approaches by hedge fund activists.

1 David Nierenberg (Nierenberg Investment Management Company) and Radisys Corporation

On November 09, 2005, David Nierenberg, the founder and president of the Nierenberg Investment Management Company, filed a Schedule 13D indicating that he and his affiliated funds owned 9.0% of outstanding shares in Radisys Corporation (RSYS), a provider of embedded wireless infrastructure solutions for telecom, aerospace, defense and public safety applications. Nierenberg's Funds had purchased the shares on October 28[3] at an average price of USD 16.24 per share. In item 4, "Purpose of Transaction", David Nierenberg and his affiliated parties (the "Reporting Persons") stated that:

"After RSYS announced third quarter earnings on October 27, 2005, we jumped on the opportunity to increase our ownership of this fine company at unusually attractive prices. On October 28, we increased our ownership approximately 50%. Now we own over 1,857,000 shares, or 9.0% of the company, which probably makes us the company's second largest shareholder.

RSYS is a dramatically undervalued growth company, which possesses a fortress balance sheet, an impressive board of directors, a strong management team, and a business model, which generates a stunning amount of positive cash flow. […] The board's decision to quintuple the size of the repurchase program clearly was the right thing to do under these circumstances. RSYS is not only attractive in terms of its extreme under-valuation. The company has an excellent board of directors, a strong management team, a well-focused business strategy, stable long term shareholders, and the benefit of powerful market growth drivers. […] Our only request of RSYS is this: now that the board has approved an expanded $ 25 million share repurchase program, use it to get the job done! The company did not repurchase shares under its previously announced $5M repurchase program. We do not wish to see the company risk impairing its credibility with the financial community by failing to make repurchases this time. Pay the price set by the market to repurchase these shares. The repurchase program is well justified by all the circumstances cited above. Carpe diem!" (SEC, 2005)

This event is assigned to the category capital structure. During the [-10; 10] event window around the announcement of the Schedule 13D filing date, the company earned 2.93% cumulative abnormal returns. As stated in the subsequent company filings, the stock repurchase program was accomplished. Moreover, Nierenberg Investment Management continued to raise its ownership in the company, as subsequent 13D filings show. The fact that David Nierenberg remains invested in Radisys until today, representing the company's largest shareholder, is also remarkable. As stated in a company news release on March 15, 2011, he was appointed to its Board of Directors (Radisys Corporation, 2011).

---

[3] SEC requires the filing of Schedule 13D within 10 days after the acquisition of the shares.

2 Third Point and Star Gas Partners

On February 14, 2005, Third Point filed a Schedule 13D with the SEC announcing the acquisition of a 6% stake in Star Gas Partners, a retail distributor of home heating oil. The hedge fund purchased its shares at an average price of USD 3.60 per share. Daniel S. Loeb, the founder and manager of Third Point, is well known in the financial world for writing public letters to company executives. Attached as exhibit to the Schedule 13D, Daniel Loeb sent a letter to the Chairman, President and CEO of the Star Gas Partners, Irik P. Sevin, in which he attacked him personally for mismanagement, poor performance, massive value destruction and violation of fiduciary obligations in a very ironic and even entertaining manner:

"Since your various acquisition and operating blunders have cost unit holders approximately $570 million in value destruction, I cannot understand your craven stance with respect to shareholder communications. We urged you to hold a conference call to discuss the Company's plight and to set forth a plan of action. [...] Since you refused for months to take our numerous calls, I must regrettably communicate with you in the public forum afforded us by Section 13(d) of the Securities Exchange Act of 1934. [...]

Sadly, your ineptitude is not limited to your failure to communicate with bond and unit holders. A review of your record reveals years of value destruction and strategic blunders, which have led us to dub you one of the most dangerous and incompetent executives in America. (I was amused to learn, in the course of our investigation, that at Cornell University there is an "Irik Sevin Scholarship." One can only pity the poor student who suffers the indignity of attaching your name to his academic record.) [...]

In particular, your $650,000 salary for a company your size is indefensible given the spectacular proportions of your failure as an executive. Furthermore, given the magnitude of your salary, perhaps you can explain why the Company paid $41,153 for your professional fees in 2004 and why the Company is paying $9,328 for the personal use of company owned vehicles. We questioned Mr. Trauber [company's CFO] about the nature of this expense, and I was frankly curious about what kind of luxury vehicle you were tooling around in (or is it chauffeured?). He told us that you drive a 12-year-old vehicle. If that is so, then how is it possible that the company is spending so much money on the personal use of a vehicle that is 12 years old? [...] We demand that you cease accepting a car allowance for personal use of a Company vehicle, in apparent violation of the Company's Code of Conduct and Ethics. We also demand that you voluntarily eliminate your salary until dividend payments to common unit holders are resumed. [...]

[H]ow is it possible that you selected your elderly 78-year old mom to serve on the Company's Board of Directors and as a full-time employee providing employee and unitholder services? We further wonder under what theory of corporate governance does one's mom sit on a Company board. Should you be found derelict in the performance of your executive duties, as we believe is the case, we do not believe your mom is the right person to fire you from your job. We are concerned that you have placed your greed and desire to supplement your family income - through the director's fees of $27,000 and your mom's $199,000 base salary - ahead of the interests of unitholders. We insist that your mom resigns immediately from the Company's board of directors.

I have known you personally for many years and thus what I am about to say may seem harsh, but is said with some authority. It is time for you to step down from your role as CEO and director so that you can do what you do best: retreat to your waterfront mansion in the Hamptons where you can play tennis and hobnob with your fellow socialites. The matter of repairing the mess you have created should be left to professional management and those that have an economic stake in the outcome" (SEC, 2005).

This tactic worked very well: a month later, on March 7, 2005, Star Gas Partners announced the resignation of the company's CEO, Irik Sevin (Star Gas Partners, L.P., 2005). Accordingly, this event is assigned to the categories corporate governance and business strategy. During the [-10; 10] interval surrounding the filing of Schedule 13D and this letter the company gained 3.89% abnormal stock returns.

4 Stock returns on hedge fund activism

In previous chapter this study gave an answer to one of the main questions: What type of activism do hedge funds perform and how can their demands be classified? However, the classification is much more meaningful if one considers the market's reaction to each type of activism. Analysing stock market returns surrounding the announcement of activism also provides insight into whether activism creates value in the target firms. These issues are addressed in the following section by examining the stock returns of companies targeted by activist hedge funds during a short-term event window.

4.1 Methodology

In order to quantify the market's response to the announcement of activism the event study approach is implemented, based on the works of MacKinlay (1997) as well as Brown and Warner (1985). An event is defined as an instance in which an activist hedge fund files the Schedule 13D (or DFAN 14A, or PREC14A) announcing 5% ownership and the purpose of intervention. The period over which the stock prices of the target firms will be examined – the event window – is identified as 10 days prior to the filing and 10 days afterwards. Further, the estimation window is determined, which serves as a period for the assessment of the historical pattern of stock prices unaffected by the event and thus does not overlap with the event window. This is therefore important as an overlay of both intervals could result in event returns having a large influence on the measure of normal returns. The typical length of this interval is around 250 trading days. Hence, the resulting estimation window covers the interval between the 260th to the 11th day prior to the event date. Identifying both windows leads to a reduction of the sample from 474 events, used in the previous section for the classification of activism, to 423 events, because stock data of some companies did not cover the necessary term of the estimation window or event window. A security is included in the sample if it has at least 30 daily returns in the entire 250-day estimation window and no missing returns in the 20 days prior to the event.

To assess the impact of events, the measure of the abnormal returns is required. The abnormal returns are defined as the difference between the actual ex post returns and the normal returns of a security for each day over the event window. The normal return represents the expected stock return without taking into account the event that has occurred. Depending on how the normal returns are estimated, there can be different approaches for the calculation of abnormal returns. The most common models are: the *mean adjusted return model*, the *market adjusted return model (*or *index model)* and the *OLS market model*. This paper applies the first two methods. Hence, for every security i, the abnormal return for each day τ in the event window [-10, 10] is estimated according to the following two procedures:

Mean adjusted returns

$$AR_{i,\tau} = R_{i,\tau} - \overline{R_i} \qquad (1)$$

$$\overline{R_i} = \frac{1}{250} \sum_{\tau=-260}^{-11} R_i \qquad (2)$$

where $R_{i,\tau}$ is the actual ex post return of security i at date τ and $\overline{R_i}$ is the average of security i's daily returns in the [-260, -11] estimation window.

Market adjusted returns

$$AR_{i,\tau} = R_{i,\tau} - R_{m,\tau} \qquad (3)$$

where $R_{m,\tau}$ is the return on the CRSP value-weighted index for day τ.

Applying the mean adjusted return model, first the average returns are calculated for each of the 423 target companies over the estimation window and then the daily abnormal returns during the event window as the difference between the actual returns of target companies on day τ and the corresponding mean returns. Hence, the abnormal returns are estimated relative to a constant. Then the abnormal returns are calculated according to the market adjusted return approach, by subtracting the returns on CRSP value-weighted index on day τ within the event window from the target companies' actual returns on the relevant day. Further, daily returns can be calculated across all companies and through time - average abnormal returns - by dividing the sum of single stock abnormal returns by the number of securities included:

$$\overline{AR_\tau} = \frac{1}{423} \sum_{i=1}^{423} AR_{i,\tau} \qquad (4)$$

where $\overline{AR_\tau}$ is the average abnormal return of the entire sample on the event day τ and $AR_{i,\tau}$ is the abnormal return of individual security i at day τ. To observe how the abnormal returns vary in each of the years between 1994 and 2006 and for each type of activism, average abnormal returns are calculated using indexes y and k as expressed in the following equations:

$$\overline{AR_{y,\tau}} = \frac{1}{N_y} \sum_{i=1}^{N_y} AR_{i,y,\tau} \qquad (5)$$

$$\overline{AR_{k,\tau}} = \frac{1}{N_k} \sum_{i=1}^{N_k} AR_{i,k,\tau} \qquad (6)$$

where $\overline{AR_{y,\tau}}$ and $\overline{AR_{k,\tau}}$ are the average abnormal returns for year y on day τ and for activism category k on day τ, respectively. Further, the N_y and N_k are the number of securities in the corresponding year and category and $AR_{i,y,\tau}$ and $AR_{i,k,\tau}$ are the abnormal returns of the individual securities i in the relevant year y and classification k on event day τ.

Finally, after computing the average abnormal returns for any day τ over entire sample, as well as for any year and type of demand, they can be cumulated over any time interval within the event window:

$$\overline{CAR_{(\tau_1,\tau_2)}} = \sum_{\tau=\tau_1}^{\tau_2} \overline{AR_\tau} \qquad (7)$$

where $\overline{CAR_{(\tau_1,\tau_2)}}$ is the average cumulative abnormal return during the period (τ_1,τ_2), in this case five symmetric intervals [-1, 1], [-2, 2], [-3, 3], [-5, 5], and [-10, 10]. The aggregation over different symmetric event windows around the announcement date is required for the robustness check of the estimated cumulative abnormal returns. The formula is adjusted for any year and activism category by summing up daily average abnormal returns $\overline{AR_{y,\tau}}$ and $\overline{AR_{k,\tau}}$ and thus obtaining $\overline{CAR_{y,(\tau_1,\tau_2)}}$ and $\overline{CAR_{k,(\tau_1,\tau_2)}}$, respectively.

The average cumulative abnormal returns obtained permit the analysis of the overall market reaction to the announcement of hedge fund activism not only during the entire observation period, but also year by year and most importantly, by type of activism, thus revealing the market's expectations regarding the specific demands pursued by activist hedge funds.

4.2 Empirical results

4.2.1 Abnormal returns by years

Table 3 summarizes the results of the cumulative abnormal returns observed on the announcement of activist interventions by hedge funds through filing a Schedule 13D with the SEC. Based on the sample of 423 events between 1994 and 2006 using the market adjusted return model (mean adjusted return model) with a [-10; 10] event window, the results indicate a total of 2.18% (2.28%) cumulative abnormal returns. Hence, regardless of the activist's intentions, disclosing a block ownership in a company is viewed by market participants as positive. Hedge funds are thus obviously considered to have better information about the quality of target companies. A year-by-year analysis reveals large variations in abnormal returns, without well-defined trends. What is particularly noticeable is the dramatic downturn of stock returns in 1995 causing -9.41% negative cumulative abnormal returns according to the index model and a similarly enormous recovery in the following year, reaching 10.51% abnormal returns. The subsequent years show unsteadiness of the abnormal returns, with some stability apparent in the years between 2004 and 2006.

Table 3: Cumulative abnormal returns by years

Panel A: Market adjusted return model

Interval/Year	All Years	1994	1995	1996	1997	1998	1999	2000	2001	2002	2003	2004	2005	2006
CAR [-1; 1]	1.77%	5.34%	-4.28%	8.83%	3.22%	-0.37%	1.80%	1.51%	2.64%	2.10%	-2.40%	2.04%	1.80%	2.30%
CAR [-2; 2]	1.79%	5.75%	-5.55%	7.50%	4.14%	0.13%	1.54%	-0.12%	3.26%	1.27%	-3.01%	4.20%	1.84%	2.42%
CAR [-3; 3]	2.14%	3.11%	-6.88%	6.43%	4.10%	-0.06%	2.52%	0.34%	1.74%	0.89%	-3.11%	5.37%	2.60%	3.66%
CAR [-5; 5]	2.83%	4.54%	-9.22%	9.18%	4.71%	-2.45%	1.90%	2.19%	4.11%	1.62%	-3.73%	5.94%	3.79%	4.71%
CAR [-10; 10]	2.18%	5.62%	-9.41%	10.51%	2.33%	-4.27%	1.58%	0.18%	3.22%	1.54%	-2.66%	4.33%	3.36%	4.76%

Panel B: Mean adjusted return model

Interval/Year	All Years	1994	1995	1996	1997	1998	1999	2000	2001	2002	2003	2004	2005	2006
CAR [-1; 1]	1.78%	5.12%	-4.48%	8.73%	3.30%	0.42%	2.35%	1.67%	2.58%	1.42%	-1.72%	1.55%	1.73%	2.14%
CAR [-2; 2]	1.82%	5.47%	-5.88%	7.56%	4.26%	1.18%	2.04%	0.17%	3.38%	0.40%	-1.83%	3.26%	1.87%	2.16%
CAR [-3; 3]	2.25%	2.61%	-7.01%	6.50%	4.44%	1.40%	3.03%	0.82%	1.87%	0.21%	-1.32%	4.22%	2.53%	3.39%
CAR [-5; 5]	3.10%	4.21%	-8.96%	9.04%	5.70%	-0.03%	2.95%	3.05%	3.88%	0.68%	-1.63%	4.72%	3.80%	4.44%
CAR [-10; 10]	2.28%	5.02%	-8.66%	10.15%	3.75%	-1.08%	3.46%	1.53%	2.63%	-2.02%	-0.20%	2.20%	3.42%	3.97%

The table presents event window cumulative abnormal returns surrounding the filing date of the Schedule 13D with SEC, announcing activist intentions. For increased robustness of the results five symmetric event windows are considered, where the day 0 is the filing date. Cumulative averages are shown for the entire period of observation between 1994 and 2006 as well as for every year separately. Panel A shows estimations based on the market adjusted return model that considers the abnormal return as the difference between the actual target firm return and CRSP value-weighted index. Panel B reports the results based on the mean adjusted return model, where the abnormal returns are defined as the difference between the actual return observed on a given day within the event window and the security's mean return calculated during the estimation period.

36

When considering activism by hedge funds as another form of arbitrage strategy that exploits market inefficiencies, then the excess returns on hedge fund activism should decline with the increased number of funds that chase attractive targets, as security prices will tend to incorporate the potential for interventions. Indeed, as shown in the descriptive data in chapter three, the number of activist hedge funds and events rose monotonically over the observation period. Yet, the results of the cumulative abnormal returns provided are not able to sustain this hypothesis, as the returns did not monotonically decrease, but rather showed large variations. On the contrary, Brav et el. (2008) found that returns on activism declined monotonically from 15.9% in 2001 to 3.4% in 2006, suggesting that hedge fund activism might remain central for corporate governance, but at lower equilibrium levels of profitability.

Figure 3: Cumulative abnormal returns around activism filing

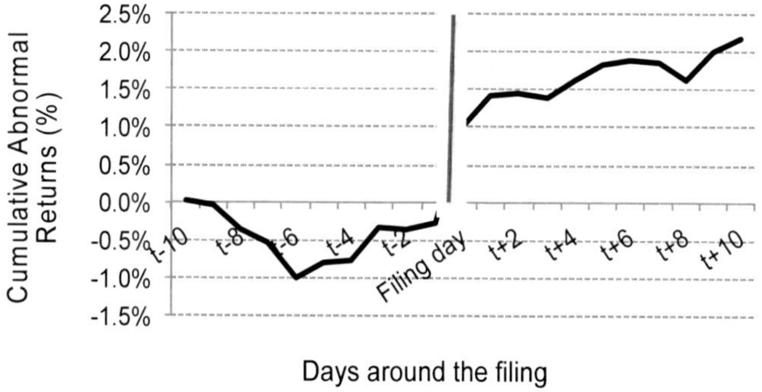

The figure plots cumulative abnormal returns over a [-10; 10] event window surrounding the filing day with SEC. The cumulative averages are computed across all events of the sample. The estimation of abnormal returns is based on the index model.

Figure 3 illustrates the results in a graphical way by plotting over the event window [-10; 10] around the announcement of activism the patterns of the full sample cumulative abnormal returns estimated according to the index model on a daily basis. To the extent that activist hedge funds seek to profit from improvements in target companies' operations, strategies or management, the increase in stock prices on the filing day may reflect the potential for improvement, or the market's belief that hedge funds have better information to make accurate assessments about the fair value of the targets. Moreover, the observations provided permit to test the assumption according to which the high abnormal return is a temporary price impact triggered by buying pressure from the filing hedge fund (Brav et al., 2008). If it is true and the stock prices after the announcement of activism do not reflect information about potential value-adding changes that activism could bring, then negative abnormal returns should be observed soon after the event. However, as Figure 3 suggests, this is not the case, since an increased pattern of cumulative abnormal returns can still be observed 10 days after the event. While the 20-day interval around the filing is rather a short-term interval, the positive abnormal returns indicate a favourable assessment of market participants regarding activist engagement by hedge funds, implying that activism is a value-adding practice.

4.2.2 Abnormal returns by type of activism

When estimating the returns around the announcement of activism large heterogeneity in market perceptions can be observed depending on hedge funds' intentions concerning their targets. Table 4 reports the results of average cumulative abnormal returns for the full sample as well as for each of the ten categories over the five relevant event windows surrounding the announcement of activism. The estimations obtained permit to test the hypothesis according to which the more aggressive types of activism result in larger average abnormal returns. The categories asset sale, takeover bid, block a merger, proxy contest and to some extent strategic alternatives are considered to be hostile types of activism. The findings show that the largest abnormal returns were generated around the events related to activists' intentions to takeover the target company with 20-days average cumulative abnormal returns of 11.30% (6.16%), as measured by the index model (mean adjusted return model). Demanding the sale of the company or its main assets also generates substantial positive excess returns of 3.23% (2.92%). These results are consistent with the above-mentioned hypothesis, since the market's participants believe that these actions can apply more pressure on companies' management to conduct the required changes. It is especially the case when the stated intentions are to acquire the target, as hedge funds, compared to traditional institutional investors, can effectively takeover the entire company and thus represent a credible threat for the management. Hence, the large abnormal returns express the market's expectations on the successful achievement of stated objectives. Activism targeting strategic alternative issues is also associated with positive abnormal returns of 3.60% (4.55%) as well as the announcement of a hedge fund's intention to block a merger, resulting in 3.58% (4.57%) CARs. Positive returns are further generated when activists indicate the intention to engage in discussions with management, to intervene in business strategies of targets or aim at corporate governance matters.

In contrast, market response is negative when activist hedge funds demand changes related to the capital structure of companies, resulting in -3.71% (-3.53%) negative abnormal returns. Engaging in activism with the intention of providing financing to targets gains negative returns of -0.93% when applying the market adjusted return model and low positive average returns of 1.69% based on the mean adjusted approach. Similarly negative is the market's response to events announcing the activists' intentions to launch a proxy contest with their targets' management with average CARs of -1.04% according to the index model and -3.47% estimated by the mean adjusted return model. Hence, these estimations are not able to support the hypothesis that more aggressive interventions result in larger positive excess returns and are contradictory to other empirical results provided, for instance, by Greenwood and Schor (2009), who suggest positive average cumulative abnormal returns of 4.56% on this type of activism.

Table 4: Cumulative abnormal returns by type of activism

Interval/ Demand	All Events	Engage Management	Corporate Governance	Asset Sale	Capital Structure	Block Merger	Business Strategy	Strategic Alternatives	Takeover Bid	Proxy Contest	Financing
% Acquired	9.4%	8.2%	10.4%	9.2%	8.9%	9.7%	8.1%	9.1%	14.0%	9.9%	23.3%

Panel A: Market adjusted return model

Interval	All Events	Engage Management	Corporate Governance	Asset Sale	Capital Structure	Block Merger	Business Strategy	Strategic Alternatives	Takeover Bid	Proxy Contest	Financing
CAR [-1; 1]	1.77%	1.34%	0.59%	2.77%	0.62%	2.27%	4.95%	4.27%	6.88%	0.16%	3.73%
CAR [-2; 2]	1.79%	1.79%	0.45%	2.86%	-0.96%	1.66%	5.10%	3.18%	7.87%	-0.17%	-1.72%
CAR [-3; 3]	2.14%	1.95%	1.53%	3.40%	-2.03%	3.06%	5.37%	2.32%	8.46%	0.22%	-2.49%
CAR [-5; 5]	2.83%	2.65%	3.26%	4.33%	-0.63%	5.24%	3.45%	3.95%	8.44%	0.44%	-8.33%
CAR [-10; 10]	2.18%	2.82%	3.26%	3.23%	-3.71%	3.58%	3.05%	3.60%	11.30%	-1.04%	-0.93%

Panel B: Mean adjusted return model

Interval	All Events	Engage Management	Corporate Governance	Asset Sale	Capital Structure	Block Merger	Business Strategy	Strategic Alternatives	Takeover Bid	Proxy Contest	Financing
CAR [-1; 1]	1.78%	1.19%	0.50%	3.06%	1.15%	2.46%	4.60%	4.68%	5.91%	-0.11%	3.83%
CAR [-2; 2]	1.82%	1.71%	0.42%	2.89%	-0.70%	2.29%	4.85%	3.22%	6.85%	-1.02%	-1.38%
CAR [-3; 3]	2.25%	1.90%	1.49%	3.45%	-1.46%	3.65%	4.55%	2.50%	7.36%	-0.95%	-2.06%
CAR [-5; 5]	3.10%	2.73%	3.35%	4.49%	0.03%	5.95%	3.25%	4.42%	6.96%	-1.14%	-6.84%
CAR [-10; 10]	2.28%	2.75%	2.85%	2.92%	-3.53%	4.57%	2.21%	4.55%	6.16%	-3.47%	1.69%

This table provides cumulative abnormal returns by type of activism, classified at time of filing the Schedule 13D. As a robustness check the CAR patterns have been estimated for five symmetric intervals of [-1; 1], [-2; 2], [-3; 3], [-5; 5], and [-10; 10] days around the events of activism announcement. The cumulative averages are shown across all events and for the various types of activism. A total of ten categories are defined, which are not mutually exclusive, as one event can be assigned to multiple categories. Panel A presents the results based on the index model, while panel B considers the mean adjusted return model for the calculation of abnormal returns. In addition, the table presents the average of acquired stakes in target companies by hedge funds, as reported at time of filing with SEC.

The analysis provided illustrates the fact that activists generate significant positive returns when they effectively put a company in play by aiming at substantial changes. Moreover, the evidence suggests that hedge funds are able to create value in companies when they see large allocative inefficiencies.

Finally, Table 4 illustrates the size of hedge funds' stakes in target companies at the time of announcing activist intentions. The first observation is that hedge funds do not acquire controlling stakes, as the full sample average ownership is 9.4% of companies' outstanding shares. The table also shows what stakes hedge funds enter into each type of activism with. The largest average percentage stake of 23.3% is when activists provide financing facilities to targets, and, since it is by no means a hostile engagement, large ownership is not an indication of control seeking. When the stated objective is to take over the target company, hedge funds acquire on average 14.0% of its outstanding shares. To engage in all other types of activism, hedge funds do not seem to acquire significant stakes, the average percentage ranging between approximately 8% and 10%. An important pattern arising from Table 4 is that activist hedge funds, notwithstanding their frequently aggressive behaviour, are not generally interested in taking control over the companies, rather they seek to achieve changes in their targets as minority shareholders. Further estimates (not reported in the table) show that the median ownership for the entire sample is 7.2% and the interquartile stakes are from 5.7% to 10.0%. Even the 95th percentile of the sample is 20.5%, which is significantly lower than a controlling interest requires. Moreover, reading relevant proxy solicitation filings (DFAN14A and PREC14A) suggested that hedge funds search for coordination with other shareholders to reach their objectives.

As discussed in section 3.2, the overwhelming majority of activist hedge funds (39%) intend to engage in discussions with their targets' management and only a small fraction of events (3.6%) is related to takeover bids made by activists. These findings, combined with the outcomes of stakes acquired by hedge funds when filing for activism intentions, provide adequate evidence to conclude that activist hedge funds are not usually interested in acquiring their targets. It appears that this new form of shareholder activism performed by hedge funds is seeking not corporate control but rather influence over the companies and that their aggressive behavior and the threats to acquire the target companies may be interpreted as a tactic to achieve the desired changes by exerting more pressure on the firms' management. These deductions are in line with the main studies on related topics (Brav et al., 2008; Clifford, 2008, Armour & Cheffins, 2009).

5 Summary and conclusion

This study examines hedge fund activism using a sample over the time period from 1994 to 2006. The findings show large heterogeneity in hedge funds' demands, which are pursued sometimes in a friendly and cooperative manner with target companies' management and sometimes with open confrontation. Importantly, the evidence reveals that hostile forms of activism are not central for hedge funds and some more aggressive types of activism, like takeover bids, are possibly used as a negotiating tool to achieve the activist's agenda. Further, the positive market reaction to the announcement of activist intentions indicates the value-enhancing potential of interventions. Activism is therefore associated, at least in a short-term perspective, with positive impact on the value of target companies. As the cited literature reports, the success factors of hedge fund campaigns as shareholder activists over the traditional institutional investors may lie in hedge funds' organizational structure and their regulatory environment. These characteristics, coupled with the evidence presented in this paper, allows to make a plausible conclusion that hedge funds could be the new forces of corporate influence that are able to perform effective monitoring of company management and possibly make markets more efficient.

Seen through the prism of the 2007/ 2008 financial crisis, some evidence shows that market turmoil has affected activist funds' performance. According to data provided by Thomson Reuters, the number of activist campaigns in the U.S. decreased from 61 in 2007 to 34 in 2008, with only two new interventions in the last quarter of 2008. (The Economist, 2009). Nevertheless, the year 2010 has seen signs of recovery as Carl Icahn together with Seneca Capital, for instance, blocked a buyout of Dynegy, a U.S. energy company. Further, "the environment for activism is more attractive than it's ever been. [...] Companies have been hoarding high levels of cash: American firms are sitting on nearly USD 1 trillion. Activists are lobbying them to buy back shares and pay dividends to shareholders". Activism is becoming less adversarial, and instead of publicly accusing companies' managers of value destruction to the detriment of shareholders, hedge funds are now negotiating with them. Estimates show that around 30% of hedge fund activist campaigns are now accomplished privately (The Economist, 2010).

Although hedge funds suffered significant losses during the financial turmoil of 2007/ 2008, with funds specialized in shareholder activism among the worst affected, and regardless of the fact that it is doubtful that they played a considerable role in causing the financial crisis, politicians are convinced that there is a need to impose stricter regulation on hedge funds. As a result, PFIARA (Private Fund Investment Advisers Registration Act, a section of the Dodd-Frank Act) in the U.S. and AIFM (Alternative Investment Fund Manager Directive) in the E.U., both passed in 2010, set the framework for new legislation, including primarily registration and reporting requirements. However, it is doubtful that these regulations will meet their purpose of ensuring financial stability by effectively limiting hedge funds' speculative activities, since more than half of U.S. hedge fund managers are already registered with the

SEC and funds that manage USD 100 million or more have already had to file Schedule 13F[4] with the SEC reporting their holdings (Armour & Cheffins, 2009). Yet, it is too early to reach confident conclusions on the impact of the new regulatory guidelines. Moreover, they could open the door for additional stricter regulations that would constrain hedge funds in their operational and trading strategies and limit their ability to engage in shareholder activism. In this case, a comparison of the potentially increased costs of monitoring and benefits of interventions could show if shareholder activism performed by hedge funds would still be valuable for shareholders and worthwhile for hedge fund activists.

---

[4] Form 13F is a quarterly report of equity holdings filed by institutional investment managers that exercises investment over USD 100 million or more in securities, as required by the SEC (SEC, 2011).

Appendix: Two examples of activist events – Schedule 13D[5]

1 David Nierenberg (Nierenberg Investment Management Company) and Radisys Corporation

UNITED STATES
SECURITIES AND EXCHANGE COMMISSION
Washington, D.C. 20549

SCHEDULE 13D
Under the Securities Act of 1934
(Amendment No. 1)
RADISYS CORPORATION (RSYS)

(Name of Issuer)

David Nierenberg

The D3 Family Funds
19605 NE 8th Street
Camas, WA 98607

(Name, Address and Telephone Number of Person
Authorized to Receive Notices and Communications)

(11) Aggregate Amount Beneficially Owned by Each Reporting Person: 1,857,291 shares (9.0%)

Item 1. Security and Issuer

Common stock in RADISYS CORPORATION (RSYS) 5445 N.E

Dawson Creek Drive, Hillsboro, OR 97124.

Item 2. Identity and Background

The D3 Family Funds are Washington State limited partnerships, whose principal business is investing in the equities of public micro-cap issuers. The D3 Family Funds consist of: D3 Family Fund, L.P, D3 Family Retirement Fund, L.P, D3 Children's Fund, L.P, D3 Offshore Fund, L.P., D3 Family Bulldog Fund, L.P. Located at 19605 N.E. 8th St., Camas, Washington 98607. No convictions or administrative proceedings as described in 2 (d) and (e).

---

[5] The Schedules 13D are not in their entire length. A selection of the relevant information is made to meet the purpose of this paper.

Item 3. Source and Amount of Funds or Other Consideration

Source of funds is money invested in the partnership by their partners.

Item 4. Purpose of Transaction

After RSYS announced third quarter earnings on October 27, 2005, we jumped on the opportunity to increase our ownership of this fine company at unusually attractive prices. On October 28, we increased our ownership approximately 50%. Now we own over 1,857,000 shares, or 9.0% of the company, which probably makes us the company's second largest shareholder.

RSYS is a dramatically undervalued growth company, which possesses a fortress balance sheet, an impressive board of directors, a strong management team, and a business model, which generates a stunning amount of positive cash flow.

The stock market has trouble valuing this company. Because RSYS is a micro-cap, not many analysts trouble to understand it. Moreover, RSYS' business, on the surface, is not easy for some people to understand. What "advanced embedded computing" means is not intuitively obvious. There are few, if any, pure play public companies with which to compare RSYS. RSYS' revenues are highly concentrated, with its top five customers generating 72% of sales in the most recent quarter. This means that quarterly revenues are inherently lumpy.

Wall Street's obsession with linear short-term results causes it to undervalue dramatically the fundamental shareholder value, which is being created at RSYS. Those who look out three to five years, like venture capitalists do, see value in a very different way than those who only look out three months.

We bought our latest block of RSYS shares on October 28, when the stock closed at $15.87. Each share was backed by $9.00 in cash (assuming conversion of the convertible debt). Moreover, the company will generate nearly $1 per share in free cash flow from operations in the second half of calendar 2005. RSYS' share price, net of cash, on that day, was $6.87, which is only about 8.5 times projected 2006 earnings. This is an absurdly low forward P/E for a company, which probably will grow earnings at about a 20% annual rate over the next five years. The company's net forward P/E relative to its long-term growth rate was only 0.4, in an industry where companies' PE/Growth rate usually exceeds 1.0. RSYS' total enterprise value relative to forward revenues was only 0.6. RSYS' total enterprise value was less than four times annualized second half 2005 free cash flow. The board's decision to quintuple the size of the repurchase program clearly was the right thing to do under these circumstances.

RSYS is not only attractive in terms of its extreme under-valuation. The company has an excellent board of directors, a strong management team, a well-focused business strategy, stable long term shareholders, and the benefit of powerful market growth drivers. RSYS' customers need the company's expertise to reduce their product and R&D costs and to speed their new products to market. Moreover, working with RSYS enables its customers to focus their engineering where they truly possess domain expertise so that they can provide maximum benefit to their own customers. Chip and chip set suppliers like Intel are driving the move from proprietary to open standards, particularly in telecommunications and healthcare, and are investing heavily in the development of new industry standards which firms like RSYS can exploit. We are happy to wait while these events unfold, knowing that the company's repurchases will further increase our ownership percentage.

Our only request of RSYS is this: now that the board has approved an expanded $25 million share repurchase program, use it to get the job done! The company did not repurchase shares under its previously announced $5M repurchase program. We do not wish to see the company risk impairing its credibility with the financial community by failing to make repurchases this time. Pay the price set by the market to repurchase these shares. The repurchase program is well justified by all the circumstances cited above.

Carpe diem!

SECURITIES AND EXCHANGE COMMISSION
Washington, D.C. 20549

SCHEDULE 13D

Under the Securities Exchange Act of 1934*
Star Gas Partners, L.P.

(Name of Issuer)
Daniel S. Loeb
Third Point LLC
360 Madison Avenue, 24th Floor
New York, NY 10017
212) 224-7400

(Name, Address and Telephone Number of Person
Authorized to Receive Notices and Communications)

11 AGGREGATE AMOUNT BENEFICIALLY OWNED BY EACH PERSON: 1,945,500
12 PERCENT OF CLASS REPRESENTED BY AMOUNT IN ROW (11): 6.0%

Item 1. Security and Issuer

This statement on Schedule 13D relates to the Common Units of the Partnership, and is being filed pursuant to Rules 13d-1 and 13d-5 under the Securities Exchange Act of 1934, as amended (the "Exchange Act"). The address of the principal executive offices of the Partnership is 2187 Atlantic Street, Stamford, CT 06902.

Item 2. Identity and Background

This statement is filed by the Reporting Persons. Daniel S. Loeb is the managing member of the Management Company and controls the Management Company's business activities. The Management Company is organized as a limited liability company under the laws of the State of Delaware. [...]

Item 3. Source and Amount of Funds or Other Consideration

The Funds expended an aggregate of $11,450,037.82 of their own investment capital to acquire the 1,945,500 Common Units held by them. The Common Units were acquired in open market purchases.

Item 4. Purpose of Transaction

The purpose of the acquisition of the Common Units by the Funds is for investment. The Reporting Persons may cause the Funds to make further acquisitions of Common Units from time to time or to dispose of any or all of the Common Units held by the Funds at any time.

The Reporting Persons previously filed a Schedule 13G on November 3, 2004 with respect to the Common Units. The Reporting Persons have changed their intentions as to the Partnership and have sent to the Partnership a letter (filed as Exhibit 2 hereto), which suggests, among other things, that the Chairman, CEO and President of the Partnership should resign. This Schedule 13D is being filed as a result of this change of intention.

The Reporting Persons are engaged in the investment business. In pursuing this business, the Reporting Persons analyze the operations, capital structure and markets of companies, including the Partnership, on a continuous basis through analysis of documentation and discussions with knowledgeable industry and market observers and with representatives of such companies (often at the invitation of management). From time to time, one or more of the Reporting Persons may hold discussions with third parties or with management of such companies in which the Reporting Persons may suggest or take a position with respect to potential changes in the operations, management or capital structure of such companies as a means of enhancing shareholder value. Such suggestions or positions may relate to one or more of the transactions specified in clauses (a) through (j) of Item 4 of Schedule 13D of the Exchange Act, including, without limitation, such matters as disposing of or selling all or a portion of the company or acquiring another company or business, changing operating or marketing strategies, adopting or not adopting certain types of anti-takeover measures and restructuring the company's capitalization or dividend policy.

Except as set forth above, and in the letter attached hereto as Exhibit 2, the Reporting Persons do not have any present plans or proposals that relate to or would result in any of the actions required to be described in Item 4 of Schedule 13D. Each of the Reporting Persons may, at any time, review or reconsider its position with respect to the Partnership and formulate plans or proposals with respect to any of such matters, but has no present intention of doing so.

[Exhibit 2]

VIA FACSIMILE & U.S. MAIL

February 14, 2005

Mr. Irik P. Sevin Chairman, President and CEO Star Gas Partners L.P. 2187 Atlantic Street Stamford CT 06902

Dear Irik:

Third Point LLC ("Third Point") advises certain entities that hold 1,945,500 common units in Star Gas Partners L.P. ("Star Gas" or the "Company") (NYSE: SGU). Our 6% interest in the common units of the Company makes us your largest unitholder. Unlike the poor, hapless retail investors "stuffed" with purchases at the $24 level (many of whom are party to class action lawsuits against you personally and against the Company), we purchased our stake around these levels and took profits on about 500,000 shares near the $7.00 per unit level.

Since your various acquisition and operating blunders have cost unit holders approximately $570 million in value destruction, I cannot understand your craven stance with respect to shareholder communications. We urged you to hold a conference call to discuss the Company's plight and to set forth a plan of action.

We have also tried to reach you on innumerable occasions only to be told that your legal counsel advised you against speaking to bondholders and shareholders due to the torrent of shareholder litigation currently being brought against senior management and the Company. We did receive a call from Company CFO Ami Trauber (who I was interested to learn previously worked at Syratech (NASD: SYRA) which currently trades at 6 pennies a share and is undergoing a restructuring of its debt). How peculiar that Ami, who is named in virtually all the same shareholder class action complaints that have been filed, is not subject to the same gag order mandated by Company counsel. Since you refused for months to take our numerous calls, I must regrettably communicate with you in the public forum afforded us by Section 13(d) of the Securities Exchange Act of 1934.

Sadly, your ineptitude is not limited to your failure to communicate with bond and unit holders. A review of your record reveals years of value destruction and strategic blunders, which have led us to dub you one of the most dangerous and incompetent executives in America. (I was amused to learn, in the course of our investigation, that at Cornell University there is an "Irik Sevin Scholarship." One can only pity the poor student who suffers the indignity of attaching your name to his academic record.)

On October 18, 2004, Star Gas announced the suspension of its common unit dividend, causing an 80% crash in unit price from $21.60 on October 17th to $4.32 on October 18th and destroying over $550 million of value.

On November 18, 2004, after a modest recovery in the stock price, Star Gas announced the sale of its propane business, causing the common units to decline in price from $6.68 on November 17th to $5.55 on November 22nd. Management evidently felt this would create shareholder value when in fact it did the exact opposite. The Company apparently did not feel a fiduciary obligation to maximize value for unit holders, and elected not to return calls from major unitholders prior to the sale of the propane segment. Had you been more responsive, we could have warned you that this that action would not create value. Shockingly, the Company also indicated that unitholders would be "passed through" a taxable gain on sale of up to $10.53 per share even though unitholders may have suffered a loss of over $15.00 a unit.

To add insult to unitholder injury, and to ensure you a dazzling place in the firmament of bad management, we learned that two members of the Company's special committee assigned to evaluate the sale of the propane business, Stephen Russell and William P. Nicolletti, received a one-time fee of $100,000 each! Was that really necessary given that you paid advisory fees to Lehman Brothers (your former employer), paid additional advisory fees to KeyBanc Capital for advising the special committee and paid significant legal fees associated with the transaction? The dereliction of fiduciary duty is truly astounding and we demand that all fees paid to the special committee be repaid immediately by Mr. Russell and Mr. Nicolletti.

On December 17, 2004, Star Gas closed on a $260 million JP Morgan working capital facility. As of December 31, 2004, the Company was already in violation of its fixed charge coverage ratio of 1.1x to 1.0x. As a result, the Company has been forced to use $40 million of the $143.5 million in excess proceeds from the propane business sale for working capital purposes in order to maintain minimum availability on the working capital facility of $25 million to prevent a violation from occurring under the credit agreement. Clearly, JP Morgan did not expect EBITDA of $0 million (before non-recurring items) for the quarter ending December 31, 2004 given that the deal closed December 17, 2004. I also presume that Peter J Solomon (the Company's restructuring advisor) was not marketing a refinancing based on such projections.

In its Form 10-K filed December 14, 2004 (with 17 days left in quarter), the Company that stated heating oil volumes were down 7.2% year-over-year for the two months ended November 30, 2004. However, in its Form 10-Q for the quarter ended December 31, 2004, the Company indicated that heating oil volumes were down 15% for the entire quarter. This would mean one of three things: (i) volumes were down over 50% in the last part of the year (hard to believe), (ii) management does not have an accurate picture of where the business is heading or (iii) management felt it was unnecessary to update its unitholders on material information regarding its customers heading into the all-important winter season.

As mentioned above, for the quarter ended December 31, 2004, EBITDA declined to $0 million from $26 million the prior year. Heating oil volume was down 15%, gross margin per gallon was down over $0.05 or approximately 10%, but fixed costs (delivery, branch, G&A) were up 8%. This is unacceptable and will cause a death spiral. How are you rationalizing the cost structure of the business? Ami Trauber indicated to us that the Company believes it can improve EBITDA margin per gallon to historical levels of $0.12 (some of your competitors are at an approximate 50% premium to that). As your largest common unitholder, we insist that you provide a plan of action on how you will achieve that goal.

Furthermore, we would also like to understand why, even at its peak performance, the Company's margins are significantly lower than those of your competitors. We do not see any reason why a properly managed heating oil distribution business should not operate at least at your historical margin levels, if not at levels similar to the 17% margins enjoyed by your competitors. We would like to form a special committee of unitholders and would like to retain an independent consulting firm to evaluate the Company's operations and management performance; we are prepared to sign a confidentiality agreement in order to have access to the necessary Company data.

The Company received $153.5 million of net proceeds from the sale of the propane business. Star Gas has indicated it has until the end of the year to make use of this cash. However, the Company must pay interest on the MLP Notes of 10.25% per year, amounting to $15.7 million in annual costs (or almost $0.50 a unit) if the Notes are not repurchased immediately. We urge you not to destroy more value for unit holders than you already have; we believe that, unless there is a better use for the cash, the Noteholders should be repaid as soon as practicable before that cash is burned away. However, if you think there is a better alternative than repaying the Noteholders, such as tuck-in acquisitions, we would like to understand that strategy before cash is deployed.

The Company's expenditure on legal and banking fees is completely inexplicable and out of proportion to the Company's size, resources and scant earnings. We estimate the Company has spent approximately $75 million in fees over the last four months (approximately 50% of SGU's market capitalization) related to make-whole payments, bridge financing, debt refinancing, advisory professional fees and legal costs.

Furthermore, a careful reading of the small print in the Company's most recent Form 10-K reveals a further record of abysmal corporate governance. In particular, your $650,000 salary for a company your size is indefensible given the spectacular proportions of your failure as an executive. Furthermore, given the magnitude of your salary, perhaps you can explain why the Company paid $41,153 for your professional fees in 2004 and why the Company is paying $9,328 for the personal use of company owned vehicles. We questioned Mr. Trauber about the nature of this expense, and I was frankly curious about what kind of luxury vehicle you were tooling around in (or is it chauffeured?). He told us that you drive a 12 year old vehicle. If that is so, then how is it possible that the company is spending so much money on the personal use of a vehicle that is 12 years old? Additionally, your personal use of a Company car appears to violate the Company's Code of Conduct and ethics which states that "All Company assets (e.g. phones, computers, etc) should be used for legitimate business purposes." We demand that you cease accepting a car allowance for personal use of a Company vehicle, in apparent violation of the Company's Code of Conduct and Ethics. We also demand that you voluntarily eliminate your salary until dividend payments to common unit holders are resumed.

The Company's Code of Conduct and Ethics also clearly states under the section on Conflics of Interest, that

> A "conflict occurs when an individual's private interest interferes or even appears to interfere in any way with the person's professional relationships and/or the interests of SGP. You are conflicted if you take actions or have interests that may make it difficult for you to perform work for SGP objectively and effectively. Likewise, you are conflicted if you or a member of your family receives personal benefits as a result of your position in SGP...You should avoid even the appearance of such a conflict. For example, there is a likely conflict of interest if you:
>
> 1. Cause SGP to engage in business transaction with relatives or friends;...

By this clearly stated policy, how is it possible that you selected your elderly 78-year old mom to serve on the Company's Board of Directors and as a full-time employee providing employee and unitholder services? We further wonder under what theory of corporate governance does one's mom sit on a Company board. Should you be found derelict in the performance of your executive duties, as we believe is the case, we do not believe your mom is the right person to fire you from your job. We are concerned that you have placed your greed and desire to supplement your family income - through the director's fees of $27,000 and your mom's $199,000 base salary - ahead of the interests of unitholders. We insist that your mom resign immediately from the Company's board of directors.

Irik, at this point, the junior subordinated units that you hold are completely out of the money and hold little potential for receiving any future value. It seems that Star Gas can only serve as your personal "honey pot" from which to extract salary for yourself and family members, fees for your cronies and to insulate you from the numerous lawsuits that you personally face due to your prior alleged fabrications, misstatements and broken promises.

I have known you personally for many years and thus what I am about to say may seem harsh, but is said with some authority. It is time for you to step down from your role as CEO and director so that you can do what you do best: retreat to your waterfront mansion in the Hamptons where you can play tennis and hobnob with your fellow socialites. The matter of repairing the mess you have created should be left to professional management and those that have an economic stake in the outcome.

Sincerely,
/s/ Daniel S. Loeb
Daniel S. Loeb

References

Allen, F., Myers, S. C., & Brealey, R. A. (2008). *Principles of Corporate Finance.* McGraw-Hill International Edition.

Armour, J., & Cheffins, B. (2009, September 01). *The Rise and Fall (?) of Shareholder Activism by Hedge Funds.* Retrieved November 20, 2011 from Social Science Research Network: http://papers.ssrn.com/sol3/papers.cfm?abstract_id=1489336

Böhm, O., & Grote, M. (2009, December). *Hedgefonds-Aktivismus in Deutschland.* Retrieved November 05, 2011 from Bundesverband Alternative Investments e.V.: http://www.bvai.de/fileadmin/PDFs/DE/Newsletter/Newsletter%202009/BAI_Newsletter_IV_2009.pdf

Bainbridge, S. M. (2005). *Shareholder Activism and Institutional Investors.* Retrieved November 03, 2011 from Social Science Research Network: http://papers.ssrn.com/sol3/papers.cfm?abstract_id=796227

Black, B. S. (1990). Shareholder Passivity Reexamined. *Michigan Law Review , 89* (3), 520-608.

Brav, A. P., Jiang, W., Partnoy , F., & Thomas , R. S. (2008, March). *The Returns to Hedge Fund Activism.* Retrieved December 18, 2011 from Social Science Research Network: http://papers.ssrn.com/sol3/papers.cfm?abstract_id=1111778

Brav, A. P., Jiang, W., Thomas, R. S., & Partnoy, F. (2008). Hedge Fund Activism, Corporate Governance, and Firm Performance. *Journal of Finance , 63* (4), 1729-1775.

Brown, S. J., & Warner, J. B. (1985). Using Daily Stock Returns: The Case of Event Studies. *Journal of Financial Economics , 14*, 3-31.

CFO. (2005, November 15). *Hedge Fund Pressures McDonald's.* Retrieved November 04, 2011 from http://www.cfo.com/article.cfm/5164215?f=related

Clifford, C. P. (2008). "Value creation or destruction? Hedge funds as shareholder activists". *Journal of Corporate Finance , 14*, 323–336.

CNN Money. (2006, February 08). *Icahn calls for Time Warner breakup, buyback.* Retrieved November 04, 2011 from http://money.cnn.com/2006/02/07/news/companies/timewarner_icahn/index.htm

CNN Money. (2006, March 30). *Novartis-Chiron deadline approaches. Will Novartis raise its bid for troubled vaccine maker?* Retrieved November 04, 2011 from http://money.cnn.com/2006/03/30/news/companies/novartis_chiron/index.htm

Financial Times. (2005, February 22). *Investors warn D Börse board*. Retrieved November 04, 2011 from http://www.ft.com/intl/cms/s/0/c9eb94f2-8477-11d9-ad81-00000e2511c8.html#axzz1cjbcjOK9

Greenwood, R., & Schor, M. (2009, January 22). *Investor Activism and Takeovers*. Retrieved November 03, 2011 from Social Science Research Network: http://papers.ssrn.com/sol3/papers.cfm?abstract_id=1003792

Kahan, M., & Rock, E. B. (2006, July). *Hedge Funds in Corporate Governance and Corporate Control*. Retrieved November 04, 2011 from Social Science Research Network: http://ssrn.com/abstract_id=919881

Karpoff, J. M., Malatesta, P. H., & Walkling, R. A. (1996). Corporate governance and shareholder initiatives: Empirical evidence. *Journal of Financial Economics , 42*, 365-395.

MacKinlay, C. A. (1997). Event Studies in Economics and Finance. *Journal of Economic Literature , 35*, 13-39.

Partnoy, F., & Thomas, R. S. (2005, January 15). *The New Shareholder Activism*. Retrieved December 18, 2011 from Social Science Research Network: http://papers.ssrn.com/sol3/papers.cfm?abstract_id=876344

Radisys Corporation. (2011, March 15). *News Release*. Retrieved December 4, 2011 from RadiSys Announces New Board Member: http://investor.radisys.com/phoenix.zhtml?c=90237&p=irol-newsArticle&ID=1539421&highlight=

Rock, E. B. (1991). The Logic and (Uncertain) Significance of Institutional Shareholder Activism. *The Georgetown Law Journal , 79*, 445-506.

Romano, R. (2001). *Less is more: making shareholder activism a valuable mechanism of corporate governance*. Retrieved November 03, 2011 from Center for Research on Pensions and Welfare Policies: http://cerp.unito.it/index.php/it/pubblicazioni/working-papers/64-less-is-more-making-shareholder-activism-a-valuable-mechanism-of-corporate-governance

SEC. (2000, Februar 11). *U.S. Securities and Exchange Commission*. Retrieved December 1, 2011 from Lens Investment Management LLC filing the Schedule PREC14A: http://www.sec.gov/Archives/edgar/data/733060/0000909518-00-000099.txt

SEC. (2001, July 13). *U.S. Securities and Exchange Commission*. Retrieved December 23, 2011 from Rule 14a-8 and the no-action process: http://www.sec.gov/interps/legal/cfslb14.htm

SEC. (2005, October 11). *U.S. Securities and Exchange Commission.* Retrieved November 04, 2011 from Filing Form DFAN14A - Additional definitive proxy soliciting materials filed by non-management and Rule 14(a)(12) material: http://www.sec.gov/Archives/edgar/data/1105705/000110465905047809/0001104659-05-047809-index.htm

SEC. (2005, February 14). *U.S. Securities and Exchange Commission.* Retrieved December 05, 2011 from Third Point LLC filing the Scheduel 13D: http://www.sec.gov/Archives/edgar/data/1002590/000089914005000128/0000899140-05-000128-index.htm

SEC. (2005, February 15). *U.S. Securities and Exchange Commission.* Retrieved November 27, 2011 from Highfields Capital Management LP filing the Schedule 13D: http://www.sec.gov/Archives/edgar/data/104599/000119312505030004/0001193125-05-030004-index.htm

SEC. (2005, November 09). *U.S. Securities and Exchange Commission.* Retrieved December 05, 2011 from Nierenberg David filing the Schedule 13D: http://www.sec.gov/Archives/edgar/data/873044/000116923205005267/0001169232-05-005267-index.htm

SEC. (2006, March 15). *U.S. Securities and Exchange Commission.* Retrieved November 04, 2011 from Filing Form SC 13D - General statement of acquisition of beneficial ownership: http://www.sec.gov/Archives/edgar/data/706539/000112978706000027/0001129787-06-000027-index.htm

SEC. (2008, April 04). *U.S. Securities and Exchange Commission.* Retrieved November 23, 2011 from Schedule 13D: http://www.sec.gov/answers/sched13.htm

SEC. (2011, February 16). *U.S. Securities and Exchange Commission.* Retrieved December 23, 2011 from Form 13F - Reports Filed by Institutional Investment Managers: http://www.sec.gov/answers/form13f.htm

SEC. (2011, November). *U.S. Securities and Exchange Commission.* Retrieved December 23, 2011 from Description of SEC Forms - PREC 14A: http://www.sec.gov/info/edgar/forms/edgform.pdf

SEC. (2011, November). *U.S. Securities and Exchange Commission.* Retrieved December 23, 2011 from Description of SEC Forms - DFAN 14A: http://www.sec.gov/info/edgar/forms/edgform.pdf

Shleifer, A., & Vishny, R. W. (1986). Large Shareholders and Corporate Control. *Journal of Political Economy, 94* (3), 461-488.

Song, W.-L., & Szewczyk, S. H. (2003). Does Coordinated Institutional Investor Activism Reverse the Fortunes of Underperforming Firms? *The Journal of Financial and Quantitative Analysis, Vol. 38* (2), 317-336.

Star Gas Partners, L.P. (2005, March 07). *Press Releases.* Retrieved December 05, 2011 from Star Gas Partners, L.P. Announces Resignation of CEO: http://www.star-gas.com/releasedetail.cfm?ReleaseID=157475

The Economist. (2009, April 8). *Flight of the locusts: Will the retreat of activist investors give industrial bosses more leeway to manage?* Retrieved December 21, 2011 from http://www.economist.com/node/13446602

The Economist. (2010, December 2). *Ready, set, dough: Activist investors are limbering up to make trouble once more.* Retrieved December 21, 2011 from http://www.economist.com/node/17633111

I am extremely grateful to Dr. Christian Rauch for his encouragement and support throughout the realization of this paper

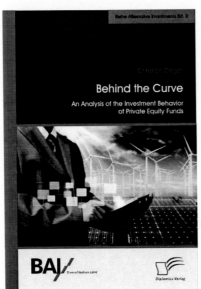

Christian Deger

Behind the Curve

An Analysis of the Investment Behavior of Private Equity Funds

Diplomica 2013 / 80 Seiten / 29,50 Euro

ISBN 978-3-8428-8910-1
EAN 9783842889101

In aviation, getting "behind the power curve" usually refers to a situation, in which an aircraft is flying slowly at low altitude and there is not enough power to reestablish a controlled flight. The only option for the pilot to recover from this situation is to nose dive the aircraft in order to regain airspeed. In private equity, especially in the field of leveraged buyouts, fund managers are regularly confronted with a less dangerous, but similar situation. Facing low fund performance or having an overhang of uninvested capital puts fund managers "behind the curve" and requires measures for recovery.

This study investigates the behavior of fund managers exposed to this kind of distressed situation by analyzing the effects on both financing structure and pricing of portfolio investments.

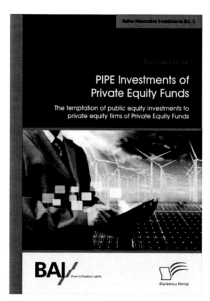

Bernhard Särve

PIPE Investments of Private Equity Funds

The temptation of public equity investments to private equity firms

Diplomica 2013 / 80 Seiten / 29,50 Euro

ISBN 978-3-8428-8911-8
EAN 9783842889118

Usually, private equity firms take control of firms which are privately held, and tend to act hidden. But, in recent years, the rising phenomenon of private investments in publicly listed companies, so-called PIPEs, could be observed. At first, this seems to be inconsistent but, it could become a perfect way to generate good returns.
This book gives an overview about the PIPE market, and then focuses on the role of private equity funds. How do they invest in publicly listed firms? And what are their motivations? Is the overall performance of PIPE deals superior to those of traditional private deals?
PIPE deals have much in common with typical venture capital deals with regard to the young and high-risk nature of target companies, and the minority ownership position. Surprisingly, buyout funds are relatively more engaged in PIPEs than venture funds are.
The author analyzes deal sizes, industry sectors, holding periods, IRRs and multiples of public deals, and comparable private deals with a unique data sample on transaction level. Finally, he discusses other possible motives for private equity firms to engage in these deals: improved liquidity, fast process of deal execution, access to certain markets, avoidance of takeover premiums and the thesis of an escape-strategy for surplus investment money.

Christina Halder

Finanzierung von M&A-Transaktionen

Vendor Loans und Earnout-Strukturen

Diplomica 2013 / 56 Seiten / 19,50 Euro

ISBN 978-3-8428-8913-2
EAN 9783842889132

Im Rahmen der Hochkonjunktur von M&A-Transaktionen beschäftigte sich eine große Anzahl von Experten aus Wissenschaft und Forschung mit den im M&A-Kontext aufkommenden Fragestellungen. Die vorliegende Untersuchung beschäftigt sich mit dem Thema der Finanzierung von M&A-Transaktionen durch den Verkäufer.

Die Zielsetzung besteht darin, die verschiedenen Möglichkeiten der Finanzierung von M&A-Deals durch den Verkäufer darzulegen. Es wird kritisch hinterfragt, welche Chancen eine derartige Lösung für die jeweilige Partei bietet und ob diese Chancen den möglichen Risiken überwiegen. Nach erfolgter Einführung in das Thema wird zunächst ein allgemeiner Überblick zu typischen Finanzierungsinstrumenten im Rahmen einer M&A-Transaktion gegeben. Es folgt eine Erläuterung zu den verschiedenen Möglichkeiten der Finanzierung des Kaufpreises durch den Verkäufer. Abschließend werden die aktuellen Entwicklungen auf dem M&A-Markt, insbesondere hinsichtlich der Finanzierungsstruktur von Transaktionen, beleuchtet, um zu erörtern, ob die Finanzierung durch den Verkäufer unter Annahme einer eingeschränkten, strengen Kreditvergabepolitik der Finanzinstitute zu einer Belebung des Transaktionsmarktes führen kann.